FIFTY SHADES OF BEIGE
Poems about Retirement

by David Mitchell

Published by New Generation Publishing in 2023

Copyright © 2023 David Mitchell

The author asserts the moral right under the Copyright, Designs and Patents Act 1988 to be identified as the author of this work.

All Rights reserved. No part of this publication may be reproduced, stored in a retrieval system or transmitted, in any form or by any means without the prior consent of the author, nor be otherwise circulated in any form of binding or cover other than that which it is published and without a similar condition being imposed on the subsequent purchaser.

ISBN: 978-1-80369-772-7

www.newgeneration-publishing.com

New Generation Publishing

Dedicated to John Midgley

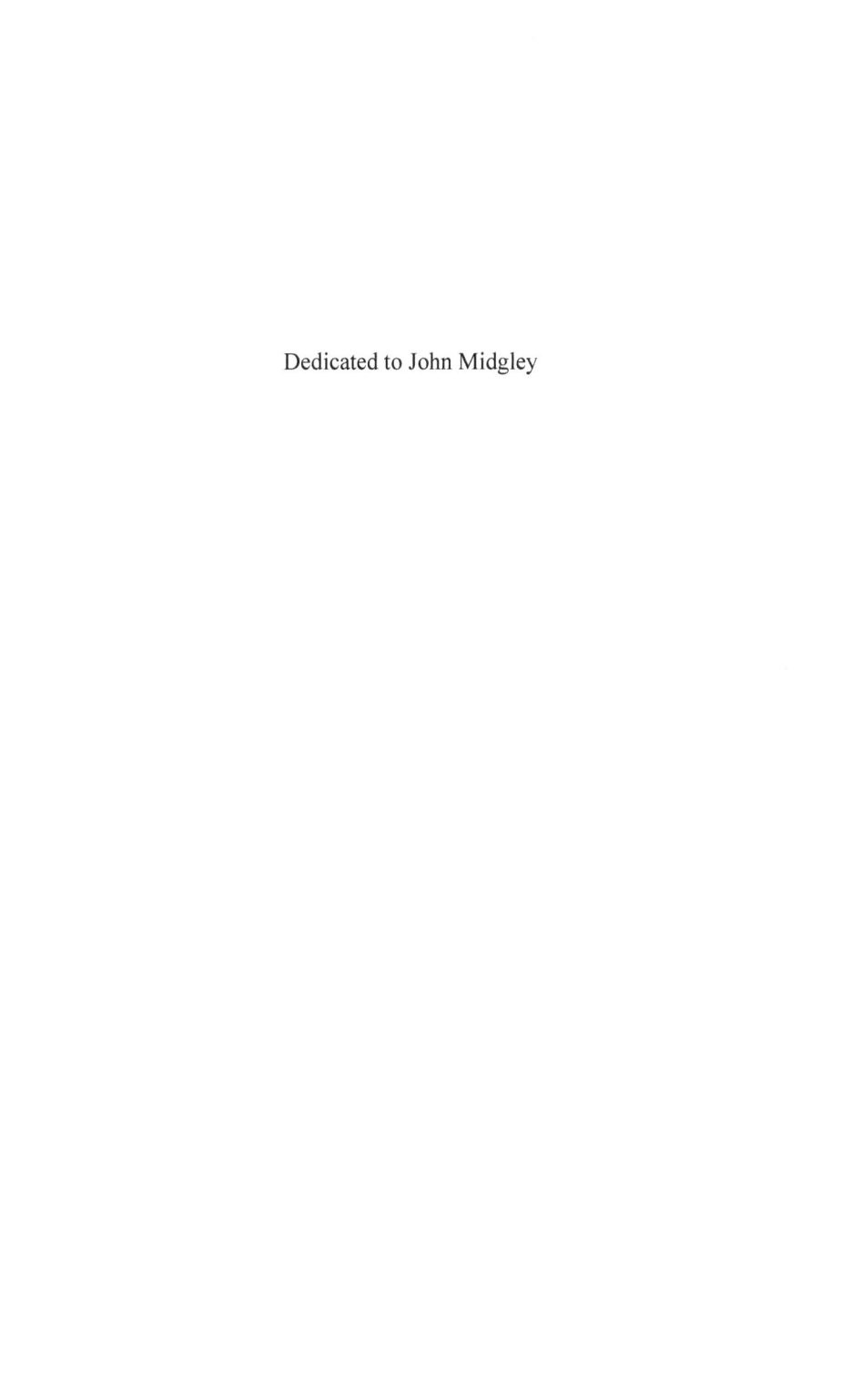

Contents

1. John 1

HEALTH

2. From Accelerator to Brake 3
3. Making the Most of Opportunities 5
4. 'Sorry, what did you say?' 7
5. Hear Hear 9
6. The Appointed Time 10
7. In his prime... 11
8. A New Woman 13
9. In the Queue 14

LIFESTYLE

10. Bargain Man 16
11. The Dishwasher 19
12. Bin Man 21
13. A Photographic Mind 22
14. Gardening 24
15. Visiting the Garden Centre 26
16. Facetime Fun 28
17. Andrew the Activist 30
18. Clutter in the Garage 32
19. Holidays 35
20. Every day's a weekend 37
21. The Golden Trilby 39

PARENTS

22 Living in the Fun Zone 41
23 Indispensable 43
24 'You're getting more like your mother...' 45
25 Telephone Troubles 46
26 In Praise of Grandparents. 48
27 Taxi...! 49

CLUBS AND ACTIVITIES

28 Watch the Birdie. 51
29 Seedings in the Birdwatching Group 53
30 Ships that Pass in the Night 55
31 Rambling On 56
32 The Gentle Triathlon 58
33 Knit and NATTER 60
34 The World of Wordle 62
35 A Week in the Life of... 64
36 The Family Tree 66
37 Meldrew Moments 68
38 Fifty Shades of Beige 70

Many thanks to Susan Mitchell for proof reading the book.
Line drawings by the author

Introduction

John Midgley inspired this book. My friend and I were members of the Wyre Branch of the University of the Third Age. We frequently chatted before the monthly meetings and discussed some of the interesting characters in our organisation. Before long we had hatched an idea for a new book. Each chapter would be devoted to an individual member. John always claimed he deserved two to himself! He even provided a title, 'Fifty Shades of Beige'! At every subsequent meeting John would ask me if I had started writing. My answer was always 'No, but I will.'

Just before Christmas 2022 John was taken seriously ill. I was prompted into action, not a book of prose but poetry. I passed on the news to his wife Dorothy and told her that the book would be dedicated to John. She vividly remembers the smile on his face when she told him.

John died soon after. At least he knew that 'No, but I will' had been replaced by 'Yes, I have.'

My own retirement began in the summer of 2009 after thirty-two years in education as a teacher and headteacher. My wife Susan followed a year or so later. Together and separately we have enjoyed and embraced this 'third age'. Almost daily I have picked up details about the back end of life and the habits and mannerisms of those who have reached it. The poems feature subjects that will no doubt resonate with my fellow pensioners. We are never far from a discussion about health. We await the next telephone call from our offspring asking us to perform yet another miracle.

John

A bowling coach without any bias
Taught me how to be good
How to master a tricky peg and
Never be short with my second wood.

As a walking companion in u3a
He led us near and far
From the back of the line came his voice loud and clear
LORRY!, AMBULANCE!, CAR!

We've traipsed through mud at Milnthorpe
Marvelled at snowdrops in bloom
Shared our love of the Yorkshire Coast
And laughed in many a room.

We've chatted for hours about football
He a Manchester City fan through and through
Steam trains gave us both a buzz
'Flying Scotsman' number 4472.

Stoical, traditional and steadfast
A loyal and dependable friend
A man of sharp humour and banter
Present right to the end.

I'm sad you are no longer with us
But dedicate this book to you
Thanks for giving me inspiration
And a cracking title too!

Fond memories I will keep
Along with Shaun the Sheep*

*John gave Susan and I a miniature Shaun as thanks after we led a walk in Goathland, a favourite part of the world of his and ours. It is still in our rucksack.

HEALTH

From Accelerator to Brake

We used to listen to rock and roll
When we were young and free
We'd sit around chatting on long nights out
Ending at half past three.

We used to possess boundless energy
Leap round at a furious rate
Now it's all changed, we're moving less fast
Held together by bandage and tape.

We chat about ailments and illness
What's bugging us, holding us back
We compare notes on the size of our prostate
And the pain from our twisted clack.

We have deep discussions on potions and pills
Update each other on jabs
Our arms are used as dartboards
And bits have gone off to labs.

We have come from rollerball and rugby

About which we used to rave

Now it is indoor bowling

Our last sport before the grave.

Making the Most of Opportunities

At seventy Tom thought his get-up-and-go
Had got up and gone you see.
Now he gets up and goes four times a night
Whenever he needs a wee.

He makes the most of his chances
When out and about in the sun
A bush, a tree, any chance for a wee
Never too proud is our Tom.

He sits on the end in the theatre
With easy access to the loo
So he isn't caught short and embarrassed
And hoping there isn't a queue.

It's an absolute pain to need the toilet again
Particularly after two or three beers
His only consolation is that his mates are the same
The perils of advancing years.

'Make the most of your opportunities'
Is John's obvious mantra in life.
When he sees a toilet he just can't walk past
Much to the frustration of his wife!

'Sorry, what did you say?'

It was mumps that got him at the age of twelve
Halved his hearing overnight.
Left ear fine, right ear not
Oh, how he bemoaned his plight.

Growing up could be really tricky at times
As he tried to cover his loss
From school mates who thought he was being rude
Awkward, as he found to his cost.

He kept it a secret through teenage years
For fear of ridicule
It was hard, it was tough, he'd often had enough
At parties, with mates, at school.

Half a century on and now he's not out of place
In the company he keeps in Perth
Now he's one of many whose ears do not work
And instead of sorrow it's mirth.

There's Jim who's got aids, of the hearing kind
While Alan's stone deaf through and through
Pete in his left, Joe in his right
Paul's hearing is dodgy too.

When they all get together round a table
It's a helluva job, enough said
Specially if Fred's left his aid on the dresser
Or Norman's batteries have gone dead.

In the end I suppose it doesn't matter
Whatever's said is soon forgot
Within a week the memory's failed them
They no longer remember the who, why and what.

Hear Hear

The world has opened up for Marcus
His hearing again sharp and clear
With the help of the app on his mobile phone
He can hear every sound far and near.

He learnt about it from Trevor
His close friend in the u3a
Who gave him a demo in ASDA car park
And told him how much to pay.

As long as he doesn't forget his phone
And have it charged up, of course
No sound now escapes Marcus's immediate grasp
He can reliably trace every source.

He has discovered that with his technology new
He can turn down the sound of his wife
While increasing the volume on 'Match of the Day'
Wow, Marcus is living the life!

The Appointed Time

Appointments are a fact of third age life
They so often get in the way
'Hi, John, can you make a four at golf?'
'Sorry, I'm at the clinic that day.'

'Hi Pete, I'm getting desperately short
For the bowls at the Spotted Duck.'
'Sorry, mate, I'm down for a hospital check
I'm afraid you're right out of luck.'

'Daphne, can you fill the remaining seat
On the coach for our theatre trip?'
'Let me check, I think that might be ok…,
No, it isn't, apologies for the slip.'

'That's the day I'm going to the Countess of Chester
To have my cataract done.
I hope you manage to fill the seat
Be a shame to have an empty one.'

In his prime…

In his prime Dave managed a million-pound budget
Kept an eye on the financial purse
His accounts and deadlines were always spot on
He knew everything, chapter and verse

At his peak he managed forty
Ran offices in Hong Kong and Delhi
Kept 'em motivated, focused and sharp
Now he can't even tune in the telly.

Dave could monitor, evaluate, inspect and plan
Relieve grateful employees of cares
He was constantly recommended for higher office
Now can't remember why he's gone upstairs.

His speeches stirred emotion and envy
His advice influenced near and far
He got to the top and stayed there
Now he keeps losing the keys for the car.

He was awarded a knighthood in twenty eleven
For services rendered they said
It was the crowning glory of a successful career
Just don't ask Dave to boil an egg.

A New Woman

By sixty-two
Shirley's teeth were new
As were the contacts in her eyes.

At sixty-four
After years feeling sore
She was given an artificial hip.

At sixty-five
She came alive
When she had her replacement knee.

At sixty-eight
Shirley's had a plate
Inserted in her leg.

Now she's three score and ten
Shirley feels reborn again
A new woman inside and out.

In the Queue

I started in the queue at number eight
With not much pressing so worth the wait.

But eight persists much to your pain.
This could be a long process yet again.

'You are now number seven.' Movement at last!
I was beginning to think that I was stuck fast.

'You are now number six.' Another step nearer.
And the way ahead is getting clearer.

Number four? My, oh my!
I've done a jump and waved five goodbye.

'You are now number five in the queue.'
I knew it was too good to be true.

Back to four, order restored.
I'm moving again, thank the Lord.

'You are now number three.' The end is in sight
Prepare your notes, get things right.

Up to number two, we're nearly there
Everything ready, all set fair.

You are now poised at number one
Clear the throat, I'm nearly on.

'You are now at number one in the queue.'
The tension's killing me, I'm all of a stew.

'Long Meadow Surgery', says the receptionist at last,
The phone goes dead, bother and blast.

LIFESTYLE

Bargain Man

Derek has an eye for a bargain
Now he's reached three score years and more.
It didn't use to bother him over much
He's really become such a bore.

He retired with a healthy pension
Lives in a four-bedroom house with wife Sue
But now his sole life's purpose
Is to save a bob or two.

He'll spend his time trawling Google
For opportunities, discount and all
It matters not what they are offering
As Derek's just having a ball.

Two for one at the cinema
With a free tub of popcorn thrown in.
Derek's never been to the flicks since a kid
When he went to watch Rin Tin Tin.

He's found 40 per cent off pizza and sides
At the takeaway just down the street.
Despite never being a great fan of cheese
It comes as a pecuniary treat.

When you can save fifty pence on a two-pound pack
Enjoy a cut price week in the sun
Get a third off a steam mop at Aldi
Retired life becomes full of fun

Our man loves exploring charity shops
Buying secondhand clothes we would dread
Leaving with DVD's he'll never watch
And books he's already read.

There's a clearance sale in the DIY
The tool section's showing a lot
He's off there tomorrow to buy a new drill
To replace the one he's just got.

He'll spend twenty quid on petrol
To save a fiver on a public house meal
He's become an expert has Derek
On every bargain and deal.

Ten per cent off for pensioners
In Iceland till the end of the week
3 for 2 at the local zoo
There's always a bargain to seek.

Change your bank and get £200
Is the latest that Derek has heard
Yes, it's life in the fast line for our Del Boy
A grade one, bargain-seeking nerd

The Dishwasher

Ted's filling of the dishwasher
Is a veritable work of art
He's useless at cooking and baking
But when stacking he looks the part.

It's one of the very few places
In his forty-year married life
Where he's completely and utterly in total charge
Even above the wife.

Pans to the bottom, plates and all
Glasses above – his decision,
Not cut glass, of course, they're bound for the sink
All done with military precision.

He's that good he's thinking of training days
For neighbours and others to mend their ways
Perhaps a book or maybe a podcast spoke
Catch him on Twitter @dishwasherbloke

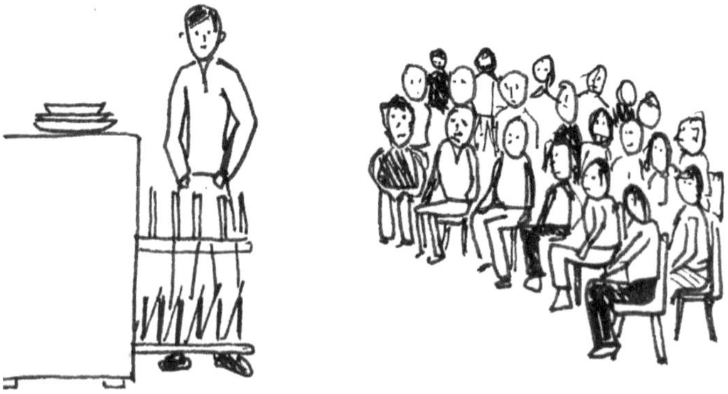

Bin Man

Alan's job is to look after the bins
In his marriage to the lovely Jean
To ensure that all is shipshape
In those containers black, blue and green.

He's written a dissertation at uni
On 'Maximizing the use of space
In blue bins during the Amazon era'
It was definitely not a waste.

Cardboard in Covid was a nightmare
He had to stack more and more
Dreading the arrival of the Amazon van
And the sharp rat-a-tat on the door.

His is the bin neighbours look at
When unsure whether it's blue, green or black
They know that Alan will be spot on
He's always on the right track.

A Photographic Mind

'Have I shown you this one?'
Graham asked of John.
'It's a picture of our new grandson,
Did I tell you we'd had another one?'

'Here's some pics of our Steph and her team,
Area champions, no less.
She's the one standing second from the left
She looks so proud…aww, bless!'

'Gemima's just had her party,
Look how much she's grown!
Can you believe that she's only six
And doesn't she look like Joan?'

'I must show you this one before you go,
Autumn with her degree.
Don't you think she looks a picture
The spitting image of Leigh.'

'Just one more, won't be a mo,
It's the car I've just been to buy.
A hybrid model with heated seats.
I thought I'd give it a try.'

Gardening

Muriel and George spend hours in the garden
As many retired folks do,
Weeding, cutting and trimming
And planting plenty new.

George oversees the couple's lawn
He cuts it as if he's at Lords,
Edges trim and stripes within
Dedication has its rewards

Muriel's the one with the knowledge
Who can tell a flower from a weed,
She makes the strategic decisions
Working out all that they need.

She walks the Garden Centre with purpose
George tagging along behind,
Pushing the trolley between ivy and holly
Finding it all a bit of a grind.

He'll never have the charm of Titchmarsh
Or the talent of Monty Don,
Happy to cut the grass then sit on his ass
With a coffee and a homemade scone.

Visiting the Garden Centre.

'Alison, how are you doing?
I've not seen you for a while at keep fit.'
'Yes, I know, I'm having problems with Joe
Now he's getting on a bit.'

'Hilda, how lovely to see you!
What brings you here today?'
'I've got a handbag full of vouchers
There'll be no need for me to pay.'

'Linda, dear, long time no see
It must be three months and more.'
'I've been back and forth to our Mabel's
Her right ankle's been really sore.'

'Fancy seeing you, Joan!
Making the most of the sun?'
'Yes, I'm looking for a few border plants
Always a pleasure to see you, hun.'

'Hi, Janice, I nearly missed you

I was in my own world just then.'
'Nice to see you, hope all's well
I'm after a butt for our Jen.'

'Twice in two days, Amy, fancy that!'
Why are you here today?'
'Claiming my free coffee.' 'So am I!'
'Let's both use the same tray.'

Facetime Fun

Every Thursday, just before eight
Gem and Steve prepare for a date.
It's the weekly chat with Pauline and Brent
Their longtime friends from Stoke-on-Trent.

It started way back in lockdown days
When calls by Zoom were all the craze.
They set up Facetime and off they went
An hour of chat was time well spent.

Despite nothing happening from day to day
Isolation very much the way
It's amazing how quickly the time passed by
None of them had a reason why.

Topics covering A to Z
Deliveries a common thread
ASDA, Amazon, Hermes too
Cardboard aplenty and items new.

'What you watching on TV?

Did you see that drama on BBC?
The one with the guy from Hollyoaks
And that girl whose married to the Italian bloke.'

'You've finished The Serpent, oh my Lord!
Don't say any more, we've got it on record!
We're still watching 'Queen's Gambit' here
But it's Serpent next, never fear.'

Political opinions are scattered free
On data, graphs and JVT.
Boris and Matt left under the pump
Then across the Atlantic, starting on Trump.

Illness, bugs and vaccination
Never a hint of desperation
The dialogue flows, it does to this day
Always plenty to swap and say.

As nine o'clock passes it's time to end
There's TV to watch, messages to send
The couples go their separate ways
But they'll be back together in seven days.

Andrew the Activist

Andrew was never one to go on strike
Being in the background was what he preferred
Now come retirement he's made it his aim
To oppose all that he finds absurd.

From the potholes on the road past the grandkids' school
To the flyover planned for next year
He's out there knocking on neighbours' doors
Without a shred of fear.

He's campaigned against the new housing
That would threaten the near extinct frogs
He made it his aim to name and shame
Owners with ill-behaved dogs.

The cyclists who used the forbidden route
Along the narrow canal side
Were not exempt from Andrew's wrath
They weren't taking him for a ride.

Nothing escapes his piercing gaze,

It makes his wife Miriam mad.
She had hoped that when he took it up
It would be just a passing fad.

Andrew's out there now, placard held high
Created from blue bin card
As the planners aim to get the diggers
To knock down a Victorian yard.

Clutter in the Garage

There was a time long ago
When Tony and partner Rita
Could park their car in their single garage
And always keep it neater.

There was a time some years ago
When Tony and partner Rita
Had a double size garage
Complete with electric heater.

There was a time when Tony
Could park his car in it
And have enough space left over
To construct a Morgan kit.

There is a time right now
When Tony and partner Rita
Have barely enough space
Thanks to older son Peter.

The kit has been sold

The cars parked on the drive
And Pete's worldly possessions
Have definitely arrived.

The garage is chokka
From front to rear
With hardly space
To store Tony's beer.

It's been like this now
For most of the year
But there's an end in sight
And it's drawing near.

Pete's finally bought himself a house
His possessions are on the way
The bad news is that daughter Jen
Is back from the USA

There'll barely be time
To restore the space
Before daughter number two
Takes its place.

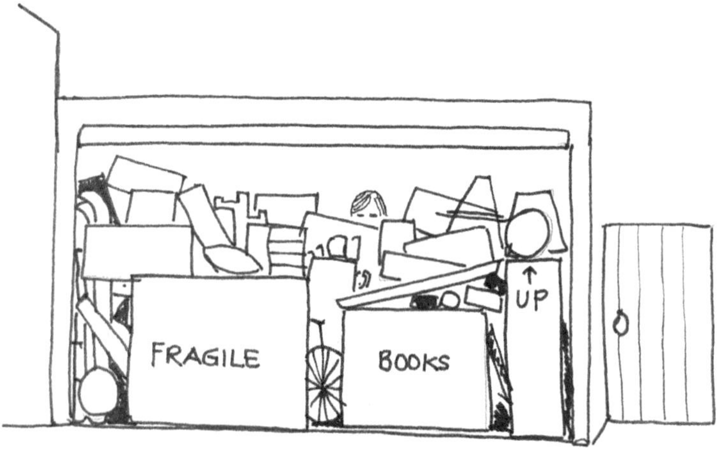
FRAGILE
BOOKS
UP

Holidays

Retirement is holiday time
For Reg and second wife Maud
They'd rather roam than be staying at home
Watching 'Heartbeat' and getting bored.

Since packing in work they've been to see
Seventeen countries in all
There's barely a day when they're not away
On holiday having a ball.

They've seen lions on the Serengeti
Whales in the southern seas
Polar bears who gave them stares
Giraffe eating high in the trees.

They've celebrated New Year in Sydney
Maud's seventieth in the Canyon grand
Seen the Trevi Fountain and Table Mountain
Everything meticulously planned.

All is currently static. Reg is bound in pot.
An unfortunate stumble in the Lakes
He fractured his foot in a pesky rut
The most unwelcome of holiday breaks

Every day's a weekend

Every day's a weekend
When you're in the retirement years
You don't have to shave
You don't have to work
You can always have a few beers.

Every day's a weekend
When your pension details have come through
You don't have to clock in
You don't have to graft
Inspect, evaluate, review.

Every day's a weekend
When you no longer set the alarm
You don't have to commute
You don't have to compete
Or even turn on the charm.

Every day's a weekend
When the bus pass has come through
It's good to be alive

You don't have to strive

Just be the natural you

The Golden Trilby

Gordon and second wife Trisha
Have caravanned for thirty years
Driving the nation's byways
Moving slowly through the gears.

You see Gordon's a careful driver
Specially with the van on the back
Slow and steady's the name of the game
Along every B road and track.

Cars line up behind him
With horns blaring constant and loud
But it doesn't affect our Gordon
He's got his head in a cloud.

Irate signals are directed his way
As each vehicle finally gets past
But Gordon remains unperturbable
Slow and steady to the last.

There was a time on the way to Scarborough

On a Bank Holiday weekend no less
When Gordon's driving reached dizzy new heights
In terms of collective stress.

The line of cars along the A64
Stretched back as far as twenty
The air was blue, the language ripe
And as for anger, there was plenty.

Gordon's finest achievement didn't go unnoticed
He was awarded the Golden Trilby
He is now on his way to Platinum status
And further angst? There will be!

PARENTS

Living in the Fun Zone

Gerald and Jan have got the grandkids
At home from eight until four
By then they'll be physically wrecked
And showing them out of the door.

Playing seemed far easier sixty years ago
Now their natural strength has been sapped
There's only so many times you can play Hungry Hippo
And you can't even stop for a nap.

By nine o'clock Duplo is scattered
Across the once pristine floor
We move on – a café is now being set up.
The mess spreads from door to door.

'Let's get the Sylvanians out,' says granddaughter Beth,
'And pretend we're making a town.'
As fast as grandad can tidy up
There's more and more going down.

Eric pops into the toy room
To find the Sylvanian barge
Next thing he spots the box of bricks
Our mess is about to get large.

A look at the clock shows it's time for a snack
To reach for the telly's remote
What shall it be? One's eight, one's three
Perhaps we should go to a vote.

Gerald and Jan sit down and chill
Checking Facebook and text
It won't be long before they are back in full flow
Gerald wonders, 'What will be next?'

They love the little 'uns dearly, of course
The times are always merry
But as they leave they're ready for a reprieve
Gerald pours the sherry.

Indispensable

Jim and Maureen are indispensable
For the next generation down
And conveniently for their two grown-up daughters
They live in the very same town.

'Can you look after Cocoa tomorrow?'
Comes the call at half past ten.
'I'll drop her off in the morning at seven,
If you could let her out now and then.'

'I've got a meeting tomorrow at three.
Can you pick up Noah and Fran?
I'd completely forgotten about it.
But I'll be back as quick as I can.'

'Can I borrow the car on Friday?
Sam's got a meeting at eleven in Poole.
I thought he was meant to be there next week.
As it is it's messing up school.'

'Fido's got conjunctivitis

And we've got the train at three
We've booked him in at the vets this aft
Do you think you might be free?'

'I've ordered a cooker from Amazon.
They're delivering it between nine and three.
We're both out at work - can you cover?
Help yourself to biscuits and tea.'

'We've got last minute tickets to see Harry Stiles
But we'll have to stop over in Brum
Will it be ok to drop off George for the night?
You know he loves to come.'

'Mum and Dad, I've got an important letter to send.
Recorded delivery, must be sometime today.
Any chance you could pop by the post office?
I'll see you right if you pay.'

'You're getting more like your mother…'

'You're getting more like your mother,'
Said Ron as Sally got up
To wipe the soup from off his front
And empty his coffee cup.

'You're getting more like your father,'
Said Sally as Ron had a moan
About getting cut off at the doctors
When he was at number one on the phone.

Telephone Troubles

'Mum and dad, I'm in a taxi
We've been to see Linda and Tim
Jimmy's face looks like a chipmunk's
What do you think's wrong with him?'

Mum and dad, I've just woken up
And should be at work right now.
The car won't start and I'm panicking
I need to be there – but how?'

'Mum and dad, I've got a problem
My computer's refusing to come on
I need it to print out a letter
What do you reckon is wrong?'

'Mum and dad, do you need the car tomorrow?
If not, can we borrow it please?
Sorry it's such late notice
But if I wait for the bus I'll freeze.'

'Mum and dad, my knee's giving me jip.
What meds should I use, do you think?
Can you look it up, check it out
Then send me the Amazon link.'

In Praise of Grandparents

Grandparents can do anything
Versatile with a capital V.
Give 'em a task and they'll do what is asked
Without ever charging a fee.

They can answer the call, request large or small
And display knowledge from A to Z.
Advice is dispensed with much common sense
Wise heads who are widely read.

They can talk with ease, charm the birds from the trees
Vital when answering the call.
Whether on finance, fridges, insurance or midges
These guys know it all.

Taxi…!

We've got a family taxi service
It goes from door to door
Door to pub
Plenty more

'Mum n Dad Taxis'
Is the name on the cab
We are the best
The service is fab.

Airport to home
And back again
Home to station
For the London train.

Down to the village
To daughters' friends
Wherever they want
Our service extends

It's our retirement business

The foundations are already laid
We've got ourselves a select clientele
But not a penny is paid.

CLUBS AND ACTIVITIES

Watch the Birdie

After a lifetime of feeling indifferent
To all things connected with birds
Pete's experienced a transformation
He can't quite put it in words.

He is now an acknowledged expert
On all our feathered friends.
With brand new binocs and camera
Pete's enthusiasm knows no ends.

He shares pictures on WhatsApp and Facebook
Of various gulls at low tides
And indulges in learned discussions
With fellow twitchers for hours in hides.

He gets positively giddy when discussing
The features of the long-tailed tit.
His eyes mist up and dampen
He can't get enough of it.

He's even bought some camouflage
Just like his long-lensed new friends
He joins them every weekend
Yes, his enthusiasm knows no ends.

Seedings in the Birdwatching Group

The A group can identify plumage
On a siskin far away in the trees.
And despite fading hearing pick out the song
Of the dunnock on the gentlest of breeze

They readily compare differences
Between various types of finch
And go positively goo-eyed as a marsh harrier rises
Tracking it inch by inch.

In the B group are those who talk a good game
But can be upended when put on the spot.
However, their middling place is always secure
Enthusiasm counts for a lot.

They will confidently pick out half a dozen birds
In a couple of hours in the field
But they will need to do more research
If group A is to yield.

Meanwhile, in Group C we have those twitchers

Whose knowledge is, let us say
More rudimentary, after all they are here to chat
Catch up on gossip along the way.

They are fine on magpies and pigeons
Know the difference between moorhen and coot
Their song book is limited to robin
But that is their preferred route.

Ships That Pass in the Night

Dot and Alan were committed to work
Holding high-powered jobs by right
Which deprived them of each other's company
Ships that passed in the night.

They vowed that retirement would change all
That days would pass by together
But Dot had a friend in the WI
And Alan took up golf in fine weather.

Dot got into bridge with the girls from Keep Fit
And also gave Pilates a try
While Alan found pleasure in plucking and strumming
Ukulele gave him a high.

Twice a month Dot took up Spanish
While Al's golfing prowess shone bright
Further depriving them of each other's company
Once again ships that pass in the night.

Rambling On

Fran and Geoff have become keen ramblers
Ever since they gave up their work
She was a primary school teacher
He had a career as a clerk.

Now they dubbin their boots twice weekly
And join others at the appointed stop
To tramp the lanes, fields and byways
In weather wild, wet and hot.

With bandages, tape and embrocation
Getting ready can be quite a faff
Lacing the boots no easy task
Sometimes they just have to laugh.

They always debate which coat is best
Prepare a flask for mid-morning brews
Perhaps a chocolate ginger if the diet allows
And a spare pair of easy shoes.

On the walk there is talk of ailments and hols

Stories repeated each time
It's what you do at this advanced stage in your life
What you are like when past your prime.

In the pub over coffee or a fishfinger butty
Legs are beginning to ache
No one remembers where they've just been
Not even passing that lake.

Fran and Geoff would love to repeat the walks on their own
With them making such a pleasant day
But what with failing memory and all the gossip
There's no chance of remembering the way.

The Gentle Triathlon

Now that he's entered retirement
Jack can proudly say
That he's taken up Triathlon
On every second Thursday.

No cycle or swimming wear needed
No massive endeavour in heat
He hasn't had to splash out big bucks on kit
And he can do it with big mate Pete.

This gentlest of triple activity
Is with the Wellbeing Birdwatching lot
And it's just what he wants at this stage of life
Because competitive Marcus is not.

The three components are intertwined
No separate disciplines here
No hard fast rules about how much to do
No sense of failure to fear.

The first element is the ability to walk

At the very slowest of speeds.
Whilst drawing in the second strand
Spotting birds on trees and in reeds.

For some the third part is by far the best
News and chat the order of the day
The binoculars barely raised to the eyes
As they catch up with gossip on t'way.

There are no times or personal bests
No winners, prizes or awards.
I can't see it making the Olympics
But it certainly has its rewards.

Knit and NATTER

Madge goes to 'Knit and NATTER'
Down in the village hall
There seems to be more in the NATTER
Than there ever is from the ball.

She sits next to Margaret and Moira
In a constant gossipy haze
It's amazing how much new they can share
In only seven days.

Margaret's op, Moira's hair
The shenanigans at twenty-three
Madge weighs in with a health update
On the state of her dodgy knee.

Stitches are dropped and row numbers messed
As the chat grows ever deeper
Margaret 's son is over from Oz
For a month with girlfriend Neepa.

Just occasionally, Kath chips in

With updates on Michaela's son
Proud granny showing off the pics
It's grandchild number one.

A pause for tea and a digestive
Then there's plenty more material to swap
The session judged not on the knitting
It's the gossip that comes out on top.

The World of Wordle

David is into Wordle
He tackles it every day,
Starts with 'adieu', 'opera' or 'roast'
Then with combinations he will play.

On a good day he'll nail it quickly
Four goes, three, even two,
On others there's anguish aplenty
Tears and tantrums too.

He curses the New York Times
For spellings from over the pond,
'OR' at the end of a word, oh dear
With those he's even less fond.

HONOR and COLOR did his head in
As did BAYOU, HOMER and PINEY,
Why not stick to words we know
Give us a break. Cor blimey!

He works out his average score

Recording results day by day,
He's a competitive sort is old Dave
For him it's the only way.

A Week in the Life of…

Monday's Pilates at half past ten
Followed by lunch in the café with Jenn.
Then it's bridge afternoon in the Three Horse Shoes
In the upstairs room away from the booze.

Tuesday begins with an energetic walk
To clock up the paces, have a chance to talk
With Julie, a friend who my life enriches
Before Knit and Natter where they have me in stitches.

Once a fortnight on Wednesday morn
I'm heading for Book Club with Phyllis and Dawn
Hoping there's someone else, with luck
Who also hasn't managed to read the book.

Early lunch on Wednesday then it's off to choir.
Trish picks me up, I do a flyer
To get to the church hall in time to test
The vocal chords so that they're at their best.

Thursday a.m's the meeting of u3a

'The University of the Third Age?' I hear you say.
Ten's the hour, no time to rest
For coffee, a biscuit and a special guest.

I need to leave at the end rather quick
To hop in the car and head for Keep Fit.
An hour later I emerge after a tiring treat
It's back to the car, time to eat.

Indigestion isn't even given a second thought
As I'm back out to an Art class where I'm taught
About perspective, tone, shade and light
It may not work, other times it might.

And so to Friday and I'm ready for a rest
But there's more to come, you must have guessed.
Line dancing in the morning, mosaics after lunch
I swear I'm beginning to walk with a hunch.

Friday evening, and a night spent in
Husband to catch up with over a gin

The Family Tree

Judith is into her family tree
Climbing it branch by branch
She's gone back to 1853
When her American cousins bought a ranch.

Once a week she joins other delvers
For Genealogy
Tea, coffee and an hour of chat
In her local pub and all free.

For her birthday Bob bought her a DNA kit
A romantic gesture? Perhaps not.
However, it revealed nearly four hundred links
That she hadn't already got.

There's a cousin in Nova Scotia,
Two half cousins Mexico way,
A Swedish great uncle, twice-removed
Related to her grandma May

Judith will keep on climbing

Back through years gone by
Until she reaches the point at which
Her sources have all run dry.

Meldrew Moments

Horace has Meldrew Moments
When he CAN'T BELIEVE what he sees
They're coming with increasing regularity
Every one sent to tease.

Cyclists drive him mental
As they take up too much of the road.
Pedestrians wearing ear plugs
Definitely trying to goad.

Those who let off fireworks
When it isn't November the fifth
Without a care for man and dog
They definitely get him miffed

Christmas decorations on sale in the shops
Before August is out
He's barely got over last year's
He wants to give someone a clout

Those pesky adverts on telly

Guaranteed to drive him mad
Interrupting his favourite viewing
To show him the latest fad.

Drunks who talk loudly at three o'clock
Waking him up from sleep
Drivers who don't wave when he lets them through
Sometimes he could weep.

They'll keep on coming those Meldrew Moments
Of that you can be sure
As Horace grows older and ever more grumpy
There'll be many, many more.

Fifty Shades of Beige

In the sixties it was all psychedelic gear
Yellows, oranges and greens.
As Sheila bopped to the Beatles each week
With all the other teens.

In the seventies she became ever more daring
Making the skirt lengths shorter
As she let herself go to Saturday Night Fever
As if dancing with John Travolta.

The arrival of kids by the eighties
Was quickly brought upon her
But Sheila still wore the fashionable stuff
As she let herself go to Madonna.

Sheila's dancing days are now way behind her
With her being old and of pensioner age
Her dance moves hindered by dodgy knees
And in her wardrobe? Fifty Shades of Beige.

Milton Keynes UK
Ingram Content Group UK Ltd.
UKHW022231180823
427114UK00010B/132